The Son of Sam

Life of Serial Killer David Berkowitz

Jack Smith

Copyrights
All rights reserved. © 2019 by Jack Smith and Maplewood Publishing. No part of this publication or the information in it may be quoted from or reproduced in any form by means such as printing, scanning, photocopying, or otherwise without prior written permission of the copyright holder.

Disclaimer and Terms of Use
Efforts have been made to ensure that the information in this book is accurate and complete. However, the author and the publisher do not warrant the accuracy of the information, text, and graphics contained within the book due to the rapidly changing nature of science, research, known and unknown facts, and internet. The author and the publisher do not hold any responsibility for errors, omissions, or contrary interpretation of the subject matter herein. This book is presented solely for motivational and informational purposes only.

Warning
Throughout the book, there are some descriptions of murders and crime scenes that some people might find disturbing. There might be also some language used by people involved in the murders that may not be appropriate.

Note
Words in italic are quoted words from verbatim and have been reproduced as is, including any grammatical errors and misspelled words.

ISBN: 9781095578254

Printed in the United States

Contents

The Darkness Within 1

The Mania of a Misspent Youth 3

Berkowitz's Return to the Big Apple 9

Taking Orders from Satan 15

Running from his Demons 21

A Change of Environment Would Do You Some Good 25

The Son of Sam Strikes 29

The Killing Continues 35

The Last Months of Mayhem 39

Zeroing in on Berkowitz 45

The Last Known Son of Sam Killings 49

The Capture 53

Sam on Trial 59

The Son of Sam Becomes the Son of Hope 63

What Really Happened? 67

Further Readings 69

The Darkness Within

This may not be the best question to pose in an introduction to a book about a serial killer, but I'll go ahead and ask it anyway: Why are we so fascinated by death, darkness and destruction? And I'm not the only one wondering; theologians, philosophers and psychologists have been attempting to answer this very question for years. We hear of terrible events and we often find ourselves repulsed and drawn to them in equal measure. Just think of the last bad car crash you drove by on the freeway. Even if you didn't turn to look, countless other rubbernecking motorists almost certainly did. So, what gives? From whence does this morbid pull arise? Well, if we entertain the words of convicted serial killer David Berkowitz, it's because we all have a little bit of darkness within us. That's why we become fixated on individuals—like himself—who have manifested a tremendous amount of this darkness for all to see. When people like Berkowitz go off the deep end and cross the bounds of normal human behavior, we just can't help but notice. And as much as their actions horrify us, there will always be a small part of us that recognizes the darkness within.

The Mania of a Misspent Youth

David Berkowitz was conceived in troubled circumstances. His mother Betty had separated from her husband Tony Falco when she met the man who would become David's father, a successful realtor named Joseph Kleinman. However, Kleinman was still married to his own wife, and when Betty became pregnant, he was not happy to hear the news. Not wanting another mouth to feed—especially an illegitimate one—he apparently gave Betty an ultimatum to choose either him or their unborn child.

No mother should be forced to make such a decision, but back in the early 1950s it wasn't exactly uncommon. Having a child out of wedlock was still considered a tremendous scandal, and many fathers who found themselves in such a situation were steadfastly determined not to acknowledge the progeny of their illicit unions. Complicating matters even further was the fact that Betty depended on Kleinman for financial support. And since this was also before mandatory child support payments were the rule of law, if she chose to keep the child, she would quickly find her and the new baby in some rather dire financial straits.

Not wanting to lose Kleinman or subject the child to financial hardship, Betty chose to give little David up for adoption. And although she knew who the father was, Betty also knew that Kleinman didn't want anything to do with the child. Instead of writing his name on the birth certificate, she listed her estranged husband Richard as the father even though she hadn't seen him in years.

Soon after David was born, he was sent to live with a married couple named Nathan and Pearl Berkowitz—the couple whose surname David would one day take into infamy. In the Bronx neighborhood in which they lived in New York City, David was known as a hyperactive child with a bit of a "bully's streak". He was a big kid at a young age, a kind of overgrown outcast, and this fact caused his peers to bully him—and allowed him to bully them in return.

Even as a small child, David began to notice subtle differences between himself and his parents. He looked different from them, and he had different personality traits. He also realized that the Berkowitzes—who were already in their mid-40s—were considerably older than the parents of his peers. He didn't understand why they were so much older, nor why they didn't have any other children when all of his friends belonged to big families with lots of brothers and sisters. He questioned his adopted parents about these things incessantly until they realized that they couldn't keep the secret any longer. When he was still just five years old, they finally broke down and sat little David down to discuss his origins.

They told him that he was adopted—but as to *why* he was adopted, they created what would become a devastating fabrication. Apparently assuming that it would hurt David's feelings to know that his mother had chosen to give him up, the Berkowitzes told him that she had died in childbirth. They were trying to shield him from the pain that kids feel when they know they have been abandoned, but as the best-laid plans of mice and men often go awry, so too did Nathan and Pearl's attempts to explain to their son how they came to adopt him. Little did they know, but the little lie they told would cause much more trauma than the simple truth could have ever done.

As he would later recall, upon hearing that his mother had died while giving birth to him, David assumed that it was his fault! Believing that he "must have killed her", he asked his adoptive parents, "Did I hurt her? Did I kick her—did I come out wrong?" His horrified reaction to their fabricated version of events was certainly not what the Berkowitzes had expected, and they quickly tried to explain to him that it was a tragedy but it wasn't his fault. However, David couldn't help but think that it was.

The Berkowitzes then boxed themselves into a corner by admitting that David's biological father was still alive. The boy immediately wondered why he couldn't visit him, and they were forced to explain that his father didn't want to see him. With the lie of his mother's death still fresh in his mind, David assumed that the two were related. He began to believe that his father was mad at him for his mother's death, and this was the reason that he wanted nothing to do with him.

It is, of course, heartbreaking that all of this confusion and trauma resulted from something that never actually happened. Betty did not die in childbirth, and David would meet her, alive and well, years later as a young man. But in this case, the consequences of the lie went well beyond the damage to a young boy's psyche. Today, Berkowitz, while taking full responsibility for his crimes, avows that his slide into madness began with this episode.

Along with his guilt about his supposed origins, David was an extremely hyperactive child. It soon became very hard for his adoptive parents and his teachers to control him. He had trouble focusing in the classroom, and he missed so many days of school that he was almost held back in fourth grade before Pearl's pleas persuaded the school board to let him advance with his peers.

Berkowitz would later say that he was chronically depressed and even suicidal from a very young age. He was also attracted to darkness—quite literally. He often felt compelled to lock himself in his closet and simply sit in the dark for several hours. Berkowitz, who today sits in his prison cell as a born-again

Christian, now contends that this was the moment that the "forces of evil" first began to take hold of his life.

Young David felt a void in his existence, and he was actively seeking a means to fill it. But he struggled to make friends, and his family life was often strained. He wasn't awfully close to Nathan, whose work often took him away from home, but Pearl was in many ways his best friend. She was the one he confided in and turned to when he had trouble in life.

Thus, when Pearl was stricken with terminal breast cancer, David's world was rent asunder. He was only 14 years old when she passed away in 1967, and he felt that the only person he could trust had just been ripped away from him. He began to turn ever more inward, turning his back on the outside world nearly completely.

He managed to hold it together well enough to graduate from high school in 1971, but in that same year, Nathan remarried and moved to Florida, basically leaving his adopted son to fend for himself. Not sure what else to do, Berkowitz soon enlisted in the U.S. Army. Although the United States was still deeply embroiled in the Vietnam War, he was lucky enough to be deployed to peaceful South Korea instead of being shipped off for a tour of duty in war-torn Southeast Asia.

It was here that Berkowitz learned to use a gun—and learned well; he was hailed by his commanding officers as an excellent marksman and given the distinction of being a sharpshooter. It was also during his stint in Korea that he first slept with a woman. Berkowitz, like many American soldiers stationed in Korea, patronized one of the local prostitutes—and it was an experience that left its mark on him in more ways than one. In the near term, the encounter left him with a venereal disease, and it also seems to have planted the seeds of a misogynist mindset that would come to full bloom later in his life.

Berkowitz was transferred to Fort Knox, Kentucky, in early 1973. Here he began to reinvent himself, and after attending Beth Haven Baptist Church in nearby Louisville, he converted from the Conservative Judaism of his youth to a become a full-blown Christian fundamentalist. As with anything that caught his fancy, in his newly chosen faith he went from simple interest to outright obsession in a very short period of time. He soon became a regular churchgoer and enrolled in every program the church had to offer. From bible study to singing with the choir, Berkowitz left no stone unturned in his new devotion—and when he was not actually in church, he listened avidly to Christian radio and spent many hours studying the Bible.

He also began to proselytize. To the surprise of his fellow soldiers, he suddenly started speaking to them of fire and brimstone and the coming apocalypse. Convinced that the end was near, Berkowitz would go around warning his comrades in arms that they needed to get right with God, passing out religious tracts, haranguing against their sinful ways, and trying to get them to join his congregation. It is unclear what his commanding officers thought of his activities, but as dedicated as he was, one can only imagine that his enthusiasm was somewhat disruptive to good order and discipline.

And it wasn't long before his evangelical efforts spilled out of the barracks and into the wider world. During this period, David Berkowitz was so enthused about his faith that he quite literally took it to the streets, standing on corners with bible in hand and preaching to random passersby. None of them could have guessed that just a few years later, this manic street preacher would become a bona fide serial killer.

Berkowitz's Return to the Big Apple

In 1974 David Berkowitz left the Army with an honorable discharge and returned to New York City. Young men were still dying in the Vietnam War, and most would have considered Berkowitz a lucky man to get out without ever seeing combat. But the 21-year-old's return to civilian life brought him only great loneliness and depression. The few friends he'd had in the Bronx had already dispersed and scattered to the winds. Much of his religious fervor had evaporated as well. He had mentioned his conversion to his adoptive father on one occasion, and Nathan had not exactly been supportive. He had raised him under the banner of Conservative Judaism, and there he expected him to remain. For Berkowitz, this was just another rebuke in a lifelong series of rejections, but it did put him off the idea of moving in with Nathan in Florida.

Instead, he used the money he had saved up while in the Army to rent an apartment. Unfortunately, as much as Berkowitz struggled to get along with others, he proved to be rather ill equipped to live by himself. Having joined the Army straight out of high school, he was used to someone being nearby to check on him, and the idea that there was no one to see to his personal welfare disturbed him. And thus it was in the abject isolation of his new apartment that his real break with reality would begin.

Nevertheless, he sought to apply himself. For a time, he utilized the GI Bill—a program that pays for veterans' college education—to take classes at the Bronx Community College. But his academic career didn't last long. Just like in high school, he found it difficult to focus on his studies and soon stopped going to class. Burned out on the idea of school, he began to work a series of menial jobs. At one point he was a taxi driver, but he soon left this position for a gig as a night watchman for I.B.I. Security.

This kind of work favored his antisocial tendencies, allowing him to sleep during the day when most people were awake and roam around at night when most were asleep. Upon coming home in the early morning hours, he made sure that the heavy blankets he had nailed up over his windows sealed all sunlight from his dank and dingy apartment. In this lonely world, cut off from society, he began to engage in what was seemingly his only real hobby—brooding. Indeed, if brooding is an art form, it was one that Berkowitz thoroughly mastered during these lonely days in his one-bedroom apartment in the Bronx.

The only break in his isolation came when Berkowitz inquired with and eventually joined the Adoptees Liberty Movement Association (ALMA). He began to attend regular sessions with the group, hearing success stories about reuniting with biological parents and learning how he could soon do the same. The group guided him to contact NYC's Bureau of Records to find his original birth certificate. When he did so, he learned that his full birth name was Richard David Falco.

This encouraged him to investigate people in the New York area with the last name of Falco, which he did by picking up a phone book and compulsively calling every single Falco listed therein. Today, of course, he could probably have narrowed things down with a simple Google search, but in the 1970s he had no such luxury. So he kept plugging away, calling number after number, talking to person after person. After he exhausted this resource without success, ALMA advised him to go to the local public library to get a hold of some older phone books. Here he found a 1965 Brooklyn phone book that listed his biological mother's married name of Betty Falco, and after a little further digging he found out that she still lived at the address listed in this old phone book.

Berkowitz was overjoyed. When Mother's Day came around in May of 1975, he purchased a Mother's Day card for his newly discovered birth mother. Inside he wrote the simple message, "You were my mother in a very special way". He signed the card with the initials R.F. for his birth name of Richard Falco, and he wrote his phone number underneath—no doubt with a shaking hand, fearing yet another rejection.

But Betty called him a few days later, and soon after their first conversation, the two met face to face for the first time since David was a newborn baby. And now he finally got the true story of his origins as Betty explained how she met his father and how he was born out of wedlock. She told him how sorry she was to give him up for adoption, but maintained that the mores of early 1950s society hadn't given her much choice.

Berkowitz tried to accept these revelations, and tried to act like they didn't bother him—but they did. Deep down, he couldn't help but feel the sting of rejection once more. One bright spot of the meeting was his introduction to his half-sister Roslyn and her young daughters, whom Berkowitz became rather fond of. He was happy to find a biological link between himself and others; he felt somehow vindicated to know that he did have flesh and blood family members.

But even so, he went back to his NYC apartment feeling tremendously disappointed. As the Berkowitzes had feared, it was hard for him to accept his mother's decision to give him up for adoption. He couldn't help but feel betrayed by the woman who gave him birth. Also bothering him was the fact that his mother seemed unable to accept the man that her son had grown into. She refused to call him David, the only name he knew, instead referring to him as Richard or Richie, the first name she had given him at birth.

Soon after meeting his mother, Berkowitz decided to take some time off from his job. The reason for this is not entirely clear, but perhaps it was just to clear his mind. If he was taking a vacation, it certainly wasn't much of one, since he mostly just stayed holed up alone in his apartment for days at a time. He only left to purchase food. It is hard to imagine that such stretches of isolation were beneficial to Berkowitz's already strained psychology.

He seems to have become marooned in his own strange fantasy world. He would lie on his bare mattress—the only furniture he had—on the floor of his apartment and let his imagination run wild. Similar to how he had shut himself up in the closet as a boy, he was once again shutting out the world around him. But for what?

After several hours of isolation, Berkowitz would begin to hear voices that told him to do things. Staring up at the lone low-wattage light bulb hanging from the ceiling, he thought that he could envision some sort of powerful, otherworldly illumination converging there. To his landlord's later chagrin, he also often felt compelled to write messages on the walls. Dealing with depravity, despair and desolation, most of these messages made very little sense. One, for example, seemed to have Berkowitz projecting himself as a king—if only a king of his own misery: "In this hole lives the Wicked King. Kill for my Master. I turn children into killers!" In another piece of graffiti, Berkowitz made reference to a "Wicked King Wicker."

Was all of this just the ramblings of a madman, or was it something more? Berkowitz would later be linked to satanic occult activity through his own statements, and many have theorized that Wicked King Wicker refers to the Wicker Man, an ancient symbol of human sacrifice most famously used by the pagan Druids.

Berkowitz's occult activity is not well documented, but he claims that he fell in with a group of Satanists in the spring of 1975. He was introduced to the occult when he met Michael and John Carr at a house party, and as we will see as we get deeper into this book, the name of Carr proved to be very important in the Son of Sam case, since it was Michael and John's father Sam who would figure so prominently in Berkowitz's warped ideology and beliefs. Berkowitz was highly impressed with Michael's knowledge of the occult, later recalling that he spoke of such things almost like a scientist.

Inadequate and impressionable, Berkowitz was ready to do just about anything to fit in. So, apparently forgetting all about his previous infatuation with Christianity, he dived right into Satanism. He began by meeting up with cult members to use a Ouija board and participate in other basic occult activity. But his involvement soon morphed into much darker practices when he began attending nightly vigils in places such as New York's Untermeyer Park. And these were not your run-of-the-mill candlelight vigils; they featured ritual chants and even animal sacrifices. The idea that a group of Satanists was sacrificing animals in the middle of a public park in New York City may seem improbable at first, but it has been confirmed by independent witnesses. And perhaps foreshadowing Berkowitz's later obsession with dogs, most of the animals sacrificed were German Shepherds.

During this time—perhaps the only time in his life that he had people he could consider his friends—Berkowitz was a kind of acolyte, instructed to read up on Satanism and occult practices. He wanted to impress his new coreligionists by learning as much about the Black Arts as possible, and his work as a night watchman gave him plenty of time to read Anton LaVey's *Satanic Bible* and other "magic books".

Berkowitz later claimed that one of the cult's rituals involved summoning demons—and according to him, the group summoned nothing short of Satan himself and then requested the Devil to anoint Berkowitz as "one of his loyal soldiers". He says that this was the moment when a demonic entity began to take hold and control his life, making him not so much a loyal soldier as a brainwashed robot supernaturally remote-controlled by dark forces beyond his comprehension.

Berkowitz has asserted that he can't divulge exact details about his time in the cult out of fear that something bad will happen to his family. But whatever happened, it wasn't good; it was shortly after David Berkowitz began dabbling in Satanism that he began to kill.

Taking Orders from Satan

On December 24, 1975, it was the night before Christmas, and all throughout the urban sprawl of New York City citizens were out and about for last-minute shopping and yuletide celebration. For most it was a happy time of year spent with friends and family—but for one lone figure named David Berkowitz it was not a time of happiness, love and goodwill for his fellow man.

Because it was on Christmas Eve of 1975 that Berkowitz first gave in to the voices in his head. He allowed the vague whisperings he heard in the darkness of his apartment to control him, and before he knew it, he was putting a hunting knife into his waistband and heading out the door looking for victims. Concealed by the denim jacket he wore, the blade was over four inches long, and he figured that such a weapon would be more than enough to butcher the sacrificial lambs he needed in order to appease the evil forces that haunted him.

It was a quarter to seven, already dark on that December night, when Berkowitz ventured out of his one-bedroom den of darkness and into the world. Although it was pitch black outside, New York's streets were still alive and humming with traffic. Many New Yorkers were busy perusing the stores or simply taking in the holiday sights of the city. Most had somewhere to go and someone waiting on them, but the hulking form of Berkowitz listlessly stalked the city all alone.

After hopping inside the 1970 Ford Galaxie he had double-parked on the street, Berkowitz drove northwest toward a revitalized section of the Bronx called Co-Op City. Urban planners had touted the revitalization project as a means of making more affluent living available to the lower classes of the city. Supposedly, even a taxi driver could live like a king in Co-

Op. But this had proved to be far from the truth, and crime and degradation were running rampant in this downtrodden borough.

Berkowitz couldn't have cared less. As he slowly cruised the streets of Co-Op's residential neighborhoods, he was just following orders. And those demonic orders were telling him to find a "solitary woman" to slay. Berkowitz felt so strongly compelled that he seemed to have no choice but to obey. He believed that if he failed to heed the demon's commands, he would face the "most awful retribution". He would never quite explain what this "awful retribution" might be, but it was apparently awful enough to get him to listen to those evil voices and do the unthinkable.

As he continued down a thoroughfare called Co-Op City Boulevard, he spotted a woman he believed would be a good target. But she was middle-aged, and apparently the demons wanted young blood, because they suddenly commanded him to keep on driving. So Berkowitz continued his meandering search, hunting through the city streets, seeking to catch sight of suitable prey in the headlights of his clunky old Ford Galaxie.

Soon enough he came upon another woman walking by herself, holding bags of groceries—probably supplies for the next day's Christmas dinner—in her arms. Berkowitz stared at her closely as his car slowly turned the corner. She had on a navy blue coat with the collar turned up, slightly obscuring her face, so he couldn't tell how old she was. But the sixth—demonic—sense that was inside of him apparently knew, and the voice in his head immediately barked out, "Get her! Get her!" Obediently heeding the call, Berkowitz parked his car nearby. He took special care to lock the doors, lest some lowlife criminal come along and steal his vehicle while he was carrying out his special mission for Satan.

He then began to jog after the woman, his lumbering steps largely masked by the surrounding hustle and bustle of New York City traffic. He was right behind her when the demons confirmed, "She has to be sacrificed!" Reaching for his knife, he heard another demonic voice excitedly declare that it wanted to drink her blood. Berkowitz obediently lifted the knife up, and then, in an "arcing motion", he slammed it right down in the middle of the lady's back.

She was wearing a thick, heavy coat, and Berkowitz could hear the fabric tearing as the blade sliced through, but he wasn't sure how much he had injured the woman. This first blow must have only grazed her, however, because at first she barely responded. She simply turned around and gave him a startled look. But her surprise quickly turned to absolute terror when she saw the knife that Berkowitz held in his hand.

She began to scream in fear, a frightful sound for which Berkowitz was completely unprepared. As he recalled later, "She was screaming pitifully and I didn't know what the hell to do. It wasn't like the movies. In the movies you sneak up on someone and they fall down quietly. Dead. It wasn't like that. She was staring at my knife and screaming. She wasn't dying."

This disturbing statement seems like a clear indication of just how disconnected from reality Berkowitz was. He was unnerved that his stabbing didn't play out like he saw in "the movies"—he didn't specify which ones—but most people wouldn't be too surprised that someone might scream when stabbed by a knife wielding maniac. Yet Berkowitz was caught completely off guard by the reaction. When he later recounted the moment to a prison therapist, he was still bewildered as to why his victim let out such bloodcurdling screams. After all, he reasoned, "I wasn't going to rob her, or touch her, or rape her. I just wanted to kill her."

This is the warped logic of a madman for sure. Did he really think he could walk up to someone and butcher them without them trying to defend themselves? Did he believe that he could tap this woman on the shoulder and say, "Excuse me, ma'am, don't be alarmed. I don't intend to rob or rape you; I just want to kill you," and she would say, "Oh, okay, sure! No problem! Go right ahead!"?

In any event, the inside of Berkowitz's mind on this Christmas Eve was indeed a dark and twisted place to be. The poor woman who was unlucky enough to cross his path had every right to live, and of course she was going to try to keep on living as long as she could. Finding herself in a desperate struggle for her life, she let her recently purchased groceries fall to the ground and raised her arms to fend off her attacker. This dose of reality was apparently too much for Berkowitz to deal with. Fearing that someone else might notice the commotion, he turned around and ran in the other direction. In his haste, he left both his first victim and his car behind.

To this day, there is still no police report, name, or other record of Berkowitz's supposed first victim. All we have is Berkowitz's own testimony, which has led some to wonder if he made the whole thing up. If he did attack a woman, she never went to the police, if she was hurt, she never visited the emergency room either.

However, others have developed an alternative explanation for the silence. The Co-Op had a burgeoning population of immigrants from Latin America, and Berkowitz testified that the woman he attacked was Hispanic. Perhaps his victim remained so quiet about the attack was because she was in the country illegally? Whichever side of the fence (or wall) you're on about undocumented immigrants, it's undeniably true that they often stick to the shadows, avoiding police, doctors, and anyone else who might report them and get them deported. Of course, this is only a theory, and the actual reason this supposed victim (if she existed at all) never came forward still remains a complete mystery.

For his part, Berkowitz was pretty shaken up after this first failed attack, and not just because of the woman's unexpected objection to being murdered. As he took off running to get away, the demons in his mind began screaming about his failure and promising to get revenge on him, either "in this life or the next," if he did not fulfill their will to kill.

So catching his breath, Berkowitz slowed down and began looking for a new victim. He found one in the form of 15-year-old Michelle Forman, who was walking alone across a bridge high above the busy New York traffic below. Berkowitz snuck up behind her, knife in hand, and when he was sure there were no witnesses, he literally stabbed her in the back. In rapid motions he cut through her back and neck, sending horrible pain up and down her body. The injuries were so traumatic that she had to grab the railing of the bridge to keep from falling down under Berkowitz's blows. She then turned to see him standing over her, and Berkowitz saw that she was a "pretty girl", but her beauty was irrelevant to his mission. He mercilessly stabbed at her face as she stared at him in horror. His demons were happy now as he inflicted this awful pain, but once again, his victim wasn't dying as quickly as he would have liked. As she continued to struggle, Berkowitz thought to himself, "Why aren't you dead?" Michelle, though, was not going to just lie down and die. She clawed at Berkowitz, bravely attempting to slow down his attack, but soon the searing pain and loss of blood left her unable to stand. She fell down and proceeded to "writhe, roll, and shriek" as if in her death throes on that lonely bridge. Berkowitz would later recall, "I never heard anyone scream like that. The way she screamed constantly. I kept stabbing and nothing would happen.

She kept fighting harder and screaming more. I didn't know [what to do]—I just ran off."

Berkowitz left his victim in a pool of her own blood, but amazingly, she was not dead. She managed to pull herself up and half walked, half crawled to her parents' apartment building. The first-floor lobby was empty when she arrived, so she tried to hit the intercom button to get help—but crumpled to the ground before she could reach it.

Fortunately, a neighbor happened to arrive on the scene a few moments later. He discovered a truly pitiful sight. Young Michelle was curled up on the floor, covered in blood. Thanks to this neighbor, she was rushed to the hospital, where she received emergency treatment for several stab wounds on her head, neck, and upper torso. Her wounds were severe, but she would survive. Berkowitz had failed his demonic overlords once again.

Running from his Demons

Shortly after his first forays into attempted murder, David Berkowitz used up the last of his vacation days and went back on the job as a night watchman for I.B.I Security. His coworkers recall no change whatsoever in his demeanor. Although he was quiet, he always had been, and no one suspected that anything unusual had happened while he was on vacation. He would speak when spoken to, and he would even laugh and smile during friendly discussions in the break room. No one dreamed that this quiet, respectful employee had just viciously stabbed two women. But his outward appearance was merely a mask that hid the horror that Berkowitz felt within himself. He was literally waging a war against his inner demons—and he felt that he was losing the battle.

Hoping that moving to a new place might quiet them down, he left behind his lonesome home in the Bronx in January of 1976 and moved into a boarding house owned by an elderly couple named Jack and Nann Cassara. Nann never had a bad word to say about Berkowitz, and even after his arrest she described him as a "polite young man" who always had the rent money at the end of the month.

But it was in the Cassara house that Berkowitz's delusions grew much worse. The neighborhood had a lot of dogs, and late at night Berkowitz would sit and listen to the constant barking and howling of these animals. Soon he began to decipher words and then whole messages in their chatter, and he firmly believed that the dogs—or the demon spirits inside of them—were directing these messages at *him*. To his warped mind, the dogs' howling was nothing short of the "cry of demons" begging him to go out and spill more blood. As Berkowitz would later describe it, "In the day, after my job at night—I'd come home at six thirty in the morning. It would begin then, the howling. On my days off, I heard it all night, too. It made me scream. I used to scream out begging for the noise to stop. It never did."

All that was too much for Berkowitz to take, and after only three months he suddenly moved out of the Cassaras' boarding house and into a high-rise apartment in the middle of Yonkers. In his rush to get out, he didn't even bother to get his 200-dollar security deposit. Nann Cassara "just couldn't understand" what would make the young man up and leave so abruptly—and she would have been shocked to find out.

Although he'd never had any negative interactions with either of the Cassaras, Berkowitz's delusional brain had convinced him that they were both evil and were plotting against him with the demonic dogs he heard barking at night. He especially despised Jack, whom he called "General Jack Cosmo" and believed to be a commander of demonic spirits. In one of Berkowitz's rambling statements after his arrest, he explained, "When I moved in, the Cassaras seemed very nice and quiet. But they tricked me. They lied. They said they were good people, and they were lying. They weren't! Suddenly the Cassaras began to show up with the demons. They began to howl and cry out. They called out the names of their masters! The Blood Monster, John Wheaties, General Jack Cosmo. I was able to sleep only an hour a night".

Despite what Berkowitz believed, the Cassaras *were* good people; there is no evidence that they ever hurt a fly. It just goes to show you how a delusional mind (or a demonically deceived one?) can go right off the deep end and create complex plots that simply don't exist. The good-natured Cassaras were surprised when a good tenant left abruptly—but in Berkowitz's own mind, he was fleeing from Satan himself!

Berkowitz moved in to his new apartment on April 28, 1976. Always afraid that someone was spying on him, the first thing he did was drape heavy covers over the windows to once again block out the bothersome outside world. And at first he felt that he had escaped the demons which had plagued him at the Cassaras' house; their incessant howls had ceased. Even so, he kept to himself and scrupulously avoided close contact with others, especially his neighbors.

One of those neighbors, a woman named Cheryl Preston, would later recall noticing just how much emphasis he put on this. One of the main points of interaction in the building was the elevator, and Berkowitz steered clear of this aspect of apartment life like the plague. Cheryl remembered that "instead of taking the elevator, [Berkowitz] would just rush down the stairs. He always seemed to be in a rush."

Little did anyone know that Berkowitz moved at such a frenetic pace out of fear of the threatening voices deep inside his mind. He believed that if he could just keep moving, they would leave him alone. Sadly, this was not the case. When a man by the name of Sam Carr moved in with his black Labrador Retriever, Berkowitz found that the dog was yet another demonic messenger. Calling itself the Son of Sam, the animal would supposedly speak to him and order him to do things. No matter how fast or how far Berkowitz attempted to run from them, his old demons would return with a vengeance. He just couldn't seem to escape from their grasp.

A Change of Environment Would Do You Some Good

Sam Carr, whose dog allegedly tormented David Berkowitz, was in his 60s but not yet retired. Still employed by the city, he was said to be a hard worker.

It later came to light that Berkowitz actually knew Sam's adult children, John, Michael and Wheat. The decidedly odd name of "Wheat" belonged to Sam's only daughter, and on one occasion a fluke in the phone book had combined John and Wheat's names as "John Wheat Carr". John and his friends had found this humorous and developed a nickname that stuck with him: "John Wheaties". Along with "Son of Sam", this became one of the names that Berkowitz would reference in his demented letters to the police.

It has since been alleged—although, it must be stressed, not proven—that both John and Michal Carr were involved with Berkowitz in a satanic cult in Westchester, New York. Some conspiracy theorists even insinuate that there was a massive conspiracy afoot in Berkowitz's arrest, and that Berkowitz was actually the fall guy for a whole group of killers, which included the Carr brothers. Adding plausibility to the theory is the fact that both John and Michael died violent deaths shortly after Berkowitz's arrest. John was found dead of a gunshot wound (later ruled a suicide) and Michael was killed in a car accident. Could these events have been engineered by a satanic cult that was silencing members associated with Berkowitz and the Son of Sam slayings?

Berkowitz stayed silent on this subject for the first few years after his arrest, but after John Carr's death he went on the record about his involvement with the Carr family. He didn't say much, and to many questions he would only reply, "I prefer not to answer". But he did admit to a much closer association than was previously known. And on one thing he was clear: He "despised" both John and Michael Carr—because they were "devil worshipers".

Berkowitz didn't say anything else about the Carrs for over a decade. He finally spoke up again in a 1993 interview for the TV show *Inside Edition*, claiming emphatically that he was indeed part of a satanic cult and that John and Michael Carr were behind some of the shootings. Although he admitted that he was present at all of the slayings, he claimed that he only pulled the trigger in three of them and merely served as a lookout or driver for the others.

To this day, much remains unclear about the real nature of Berkowitz's relationship with the Carr family. Either something very sinister was going on—or Berkowitz was simply imagining the whole thing.

At any rate, shortly after moving into his new apartment, Berkowitz decided to head to Florida to meet up with his adoptive father Nathan. He arrived in Boynton Beach in May of 1976, but it was a brief reunion, with Berkowitz only sticking around for about a week. Quickly becoming dissatisfied with the situation in Nathan's home, he spent most of that week at singles bars trying to pick up women. He wasn't very successful, and years later he would be vaguely remembered as just an odd, lonely visitor drinking alone in the corner.

Berkowitz then headed west to Houston, Texas, where an old Army buddy named Billy Dan Parker lived. He showed up at the house where Billy Dan and his mother lived on June 5th, pretty much out of the blue; he announced his arrival by way of a payphone on the side of the road just before he got there. Billy Dan was more than happy to entertain his old friend, however, telling Berkowitz, "We'll be glad to put you up. My mom likes to meet my Army buddies. Dave, she'll really make you feel at home." Berkowitz ended up staying in Houston for about a month. He enjoyed life in Texas, and he even considered moving there for good.

Berkowitz had already tried to murder at least one woman last Christmas Eve, but perhaps he hadn't yet reached the point of no return. Maybe if he had chosen to stay in Texas with his friend Billy Dan, he could have turned over a new leaf. Berkowitz himself seems to have thought that the change in environment was doing him a world of good. The demonic chatter that had haunted him in New York was not present during his time in Texas, and for a fleeting moment, he began to think that he was finally free from his demons.

But he didn't have any luck finding a job in Texas. Almost every position he looked up in the classifieds required either a degree or some kind of specialized training that he did not have. And so, after several weeks at the Parker house, he decided that it would be best to head back to New York.

But he didn't leave before he procured a deadly souvenir from his time in Texas—a .44 caliber Bulldog revolver. On June 12th, he convinced Billy Dan to take him to the Spring Branch Jewelry & Loan Pawn Shop and buy the firearm for him.

Berkowitz claimed that he wanted the gun for protection during his long ride back to New York, but the real motive behind the purchase is anyone's guess. Could the seeds of the Son of Sam shootings already have sprouted in his mind? Were demonic forces influencing his actions when he bought the murder weapon? Or then again, had the Carrs' satanic cult placed a purchase order?

Whatever the case may be, Billy Dan bought the weapon and a box of ammunition for around $130, no questions asked. After they left the gun shop, Billy Dan handed the gun to Berkowitz right there in the parking lot. No one knows just what was playing through his mind, but Berkowitz inspected the weapon and smiled in approval.

This gun would indeed eventually become the murder weapon in the Son of Sam killings. Armed with his new instrument of death, Berkowitz left the Parkers on June 12th to head back to New York.

The Son of Sam Strikes

Upon returning to New York in the summer of 1976, Berkowitz initially worked as a cab driver in the Bronx. Shortly afterward he got a job as a sheet metal worker at a Westchester County industrial plant called Wolf and Munier of Elmsford. His coworkers there remembered him as a quiet loner who occasionally got emotional and was sometimes seen breaking into tears.

On July 28th, after putting in another hard day at the plant, Berkowitz decided to renew his attempts at murder. He got in his car with his brand-new Bulldog revolver and began driving the city streets looking for a victim. As the voice in his head called for blood, Berkowitz headed for the Bronx, waiting for his opportunity. After circling around for a while, he came upon a couple of female friends seated in a parked car.

They were 18-year-old Donna Lauria and 19-year-old Jody Valenti. The girls had just come back from a meal at a restaurant called the Chateau Pelham. Donna was working as a medical technician and Jody was studying to be a nurse. Both had big dreams of helping others and giving back to the community—but they probably never dreamed about the horrendous act of violence that was soon to befall them.

Berkowitz parked his car a short distance away and made a beeline for the girls. It was around one in the morning. Donna had opened up the passenger side door and was getting ready to say goodbye to her friend and head into her parents' apartment building when she saw Berkowitz standing just a few feet away. She gasped to her friend, "Who is this guy? What does he want?"

Sadly, this was the last thing she would ever say, because Berkowitz unloaded his Bulldog revolver into the car immediately thereafter. He fired a total of five times, shattering the glass all around the girls. Donna lifted an arm to defend herself in a split-second reaction just before a bullet sliced through her throat. The impact sent her spinning out of the car to slump on the ground. Jody, seated next to her, was struck in the thigh. She reflexively jerked forward and hit the car's horn while letting out a chilling scream.

Berkowitz, who still didn't care too much for the screaming part, decided to flee the scene at this point. He ran back to his waiting Ford Galaxie and sped off. In his haste, he was not sure if he had killed anyone. Yet deep down, he sensed that the demons were pleased, and he took this to mean that at least one of the girls was dead.

Donna did indeed die shortly after receiving the wound to her throat. Her father heard the commotion and ran outside to find his daughter bleeding to death on the ground. He called an ambulance and sat by her side as she passed away during the ride to the hospital. Jody survived, but she would be both physically and mentally scarred for life.

Berkowitz melted back into the shadows and soon took a new job as a postal worker. As usual, employees at the post office remembered Berkowitz (if they remembered him at all) as a quiet and unassuming figure.

Berkowitz lay low for a few months, and then, on October 23rd, he chose his next victims: 18-year-old Rosemary Keenan and her 20-year-old boyfriend Carl Denaro. The couple had just gotten back from a Queens bar called Pecks, and like Donna and Jody, they had pulled over in a residential neighborhood to talk before they parted company. Rosemary was the driver and

Carl was in the passenger seat. Shortly into their conversation, Rosemary noticed a man jogging in the darkness. At 1:30 in the morning, the sight immediately set off alarm bells. Who jogs at such an hour?

And just moments after Rosemary sighted this "jogger", the bullets began to fly and glass shattered in every direction. Buffeted by the glass, the couple didn't quite know what was happening at first. It wasn't until a bullet grazed Carl's head that they realized they were being shot at. With blood pouring from his head wound, Carl screamed at Rosemary to "Get out of here!" She struggled with the ignition, but fortunately got the car moving and drove the short distance back to Pecks pub. Here the wounded Carl passed out before being rushed to a hospital, but despite the injury both Carl and Rosemary had survived their encounter with the Son of Sam.

Berkowitz next struck in the cold air of November 27th, and once again his victims were exceedingly young: 18-year-old Joanne Lomino and 16-year-old Donna DeMasi. The two had just caught a movie at a local theater before heading back to Joanne's house in Queens. It was a trek that would take them through the subway system and across town on a city bus after hours before they walked the rest of the way. And while the very idea of two young women braving the mean streets of 1970s New York City late at night might seem like a recipe for disaster, Joanne and Donna were not accosted at any point during their journey: They were actually attacked on the porch of Joanne's own home.

They were happily talking about their plans for the upcoming Christmas holiday when they noticed a stranger wandering around in the neighborhood. He appeared to be lost, especially when he stopped in front of the girls and asked them, "Can you tell me how to get—?"

It turned out, though, that the question was just a distraction, because in midsentence he pulled the Bulldog revolver out of his coat and mercilessly opened fire. Joanne was hit first, with one of the Bulldog's heavy bullets shattering her spine and lodging in her lung. Donna, sitting on a porch step, took a slug in her neck. Both of them were knocked right off the porch by the powerful blasts, falling into the shrubbery below. This probably saved their lives, because once they fell off the brightly lit porch Berkowitz began to shoot almost at random, hitting the front of the house and shattering a living room window before retreating from the scene.

Donna's neck injury proved to be just a flesh wound that had miraculously missed her spine, jugular veins and airway. Joanne did not fare as well, ending up in a wheelchair paralyzed from the waist down. But both girls got a pretty clear look at their attacker as he stood in the light of the street lamps, and as soon as they were able they helped police sketch artists to draw his likeness.

Strangely, the sketches created in these sessions are drastically different from other eyewitness accounts of Berkowitz. Whereas other victims described him as being heavy, with black curly hair, Donna and Joanne maintained that their attacker was fit and trim, with blond hair. Berkowitz could, of course, have been wearing a wig during this attack, but that still wouldn't explain how he could appear to have a much lighter build than in other incidents.

Now, remember that Berkowitz later claimed to have had accomplices, stating that he was not the trigger man in every shooting. Well, here are two witnesses who seem to give some support to that claim. So keep in mind that even though—both for the sake of simplicity and because he did originally plead guilty to all of the attacks he was charged with—this book consistently refers to Berkowitz as the sole shooter, there is indeed some conflicting testimony. Nevertheless, unless and until proven otherwise, he will go down in history as the lone gunman in the Son of Sam slayings.

After this latest murder attempt, Berkowitz took the holidays off and didn't strike again until January 30, 1977. His target was 26-year-old Austrian immigrant Christine Freund, who worked as a secretary in Manhattan. She was out for an evening with her 30-year-old fiancé John Diel when Berkowitz's bullets struck.

John had simply been warming up the car before heading to their destination when several rounds poured into the vehicle. Immediately thinking of his fiancée's safety, John shouted, "Chris! Chris!" as he shoved her down in the seat. But a bullet struck her all the same, hitting her in the shoulder and lodging in her back. When the shooting ceased, John was unharmed but Christine was fading fast. The wound was severe and she was losing large amounts of blood.

In a panic, John jumped out of the car and flagged down a motorist for help. But after the driver saw the injured girl, he fled the scene. John then saw a man entering the nearby Forest Hills Inn and shouted in his direction, "Mister! Mister! They shot her! They shot my girl!" But this man didn't want to get involved either. He ignored John and went about his business. It has often been said that one flaw of big city life is that everyone tends to be a little detached and unwilling to render assistance, and this case appears to prove it! With no one coming to help him, John went back to the car, got behind the wheel and parked it right in the middle of the road. Interrupting the traffic flow finally brought him the attention he needed, and Christine Freund was rushed to the hospital.

Sadly, she passed away there at around four in the morning. The Son of Sam had claimed yet another victim.

The Killing Continues

After the death of Christine Freud, David Berkowitz once again retreated from the world for a time. The demonic bloodlust that drove him seemed to be temporarily satiated. But it wouldn't be long before it started tormenting him again. By March of 1977, he was already back out on the streets looking for another victim, and on the evening of March 8th, he ended up crossing paths with a young girl named Amy Johnson.

It was just past seven, and she was engaging in her daily ritual of jogging around the block accompanied by her 13-year-old brother Tony. The two traveled a familiar route, and the jaunt just happened to take them right past the place where Christine Freund had been shot just a few months before. In a crime-ridden city like 1970s New York, a few months was enough time for even murder to begin to fade from memory. But as Amy jogged by, she couldn't help stealing a glance and wondering just what had happened to the poor girl who was shot.

Shortly after this, she noticed a man standing at the intersection of Dartmouth and Continental Avenue. Dressed in a large raincoat, with his hands in his pockets, just shuffling about on the corner, the man seemed decidedly out of place. Even worse, he was watching her intently, and as she drew nearer, she could see and "eerie, threatening" expression on his face.

Amy urged her brother to pass him quickly, and then they both jogged away from the madman, keeping to the middle of the road and staying under the full illumination of the street lights. Circling back, they would soon reach the safety of their house. But just before they did, Amy was startled to see the same man just ahead of her. Berkowitz seemed like a bogeyman out of some horror movie, possessed of supernatural powers that enabled him to stay one step ahead of his victims.

Of course, some people argue that this aspect of Amy's encounter is more evidence that Berkowitz had accomplices, but Amy has always maintained that it was the same man she saw in both locations. Perhaps the simplest explanation is that as soon as Amy and Tony ran past him, Berkowitz hopped into his Ford Galaxie and quickly rounded the corner to intercept them.

At any rate, fortunately for the siblings and unbeknownst to Berkowitz, their home was within reach. The hateful net he had cast to ensnare them was a bit too wide. As she and Tony ran into the house, Amy cast a look back and saw that the man was now walking away from them, slinking back into the shadows from whence he had come.

But Berkowitz was still on the prowl, and sadly, he would find a new victim that night in the form of 19-year-old college student Virginia Voskerichian. Those who knew her described Virginia as happy and full of life. Her family had moved to the U.S. from Bulgaria when she was 11 years old. She was smart and a good student and had already put in a couple of semesters at Queens College before enrolling at Barnard College at Columbia as a political science and Russian language major. She was walking back from class that evening just a short while after Amy encountered her leering bogeyman.

Berkowitz was frustrated that he had failed to ensnare Amy, but now Virginia was walking right into his trap. She saw him approach her on the sidewalk and moved to the right so he could pass. But Berkowitz had already marked her for murder, and he had no intention of passing her by. As he neared, she glanced at him just in time to see that he was pointing a gun right at her. Screaming in fear, she made a vain attempt to shield herself with one of the textbooks she was carrying. But this was completely futile against the massive .44 slug that launched out of Berkowitz's Bulldog revolver. The bullet blasted through the book and hit Virginia full in the face, knocking out teeth before lodging at the top of her spine and disintegrating part of her spinal column. She died almost instantaneously and collapsed into some nearby bushes.

Berkowitz was elated to fulfill the will of the demons that haunted him. He had once again satiated their bloodlust. But this time, he would not make a clean getaway. As he was running out of the neighborhood, a resident who'd heard the gunshot was coming to investigate, and they bumped right into each other. The witness later described the assailant as short and stocky, around 16 to 18 years old. Berkowitz was 23 at the time, but the witness's mistake is understandable. Old photos and old acquaintances agree that Berkowitz had a very youthful face back then. Those who knew him often described his chubby, "cherubic" baby face as making him appear much younger than he actually was.

Virginia was beloved by all who knew her, and her senseless killing sparked immediate outrage. Soon enough, the media began speculating that the previous killing of Donna Lauria and the recent slaying of Virginia Voskerichian had been perpetrated by the same man. New York City Mayor Abraham Beame then announced that the NYPD ballistics lab had indeed discovered that both girls had been killed by the same gun, a .44 caliber pistol of some kind.

This led to Berkowitz's first nickname as the media began calling him the ".44 Caliber Killer". Berkowitz—although not yet known by his real name, or even the more famous Son of Sam moniker—was now making headlines all over the world. The misfit who was nobody had become infamous through the terror he was singlehandedly inflicting on a helpless city.

The Last Months of Mayhem

I SAY GOODBYE AND GOODNIGHT.

POLICE: LET ME HAUNT YOU WITH THESE WORDS;

I'LL BE BACK!
I'LL BE BACK!

TO BE INTERRPRETED AS - BANG BANG BANG BANG, BANG - UGH!!

YOURS IN MURDER
MR. MONSTER

Berkowitz found his next victims on April 17, 1977, when 20-year-old Alexander Esau attempted to drop off his girlfriend, 18-year-old Valentina Suriani, at her home in the Bronx. They had taken in a movie earlier in the evening and then spent some time at a party at a friend's house before parking in front of Valentina's home. Like most young couples who still lived with their parents, Alex and Valentina always made the most of their goodbyes, since they knew that the privacy of an automobile was the best they could manage.

On this night Alex was driving a Mercury Montego he had borrowed from his brother. It was a fairly spacious car, and the couple relished the comfort it provided as they moved closer to each other. This was their long-awaited alone time. But sadly, they were not as alone as they thought they were that night—Berkowitz was waiting for them. As Valentina positioned herself on Alex's lap and the two passionately made out, Berkowitz was aiming his weapon and getting ready to fire.

The couple's lips were lovingly pressed together when Berkowitz's hateful bullet literally came between them, striking Valentina in the left corner of her mouth. This slug then passed through her head before rocketing out of her right ear. A second shot rang out and another bullet slammed into the left side of Valentina's head, killing her instantly as her body still clung to her bewildered boyfriend.

Everything had happened so fast—in just a matter of seconds—that Alex couldn't process it. Still clinging to Valentina, he instinctively ducked forward, but this motion actually brought him into the line of fire. He took two shots to the head and didn't move another muscle after that. Both he and Valentina lay locked in their last embrace. Alex was barely alive when they were discovered, but this weak spark of life quickly dissipated and he was pronounced dead just a few hours later.

This was yet another seemingly random—yet somehow related—slaying in New York by a lone, unknown gunman. The circumstances were sickeningly similar to all the rest, but there was one notable difference this time around: The killer decided to leave a calling card. At the scene of the grisly murders of Alex Esau and Valentina Suriani, Berkowitz left a note taunting investigators about their efforts to track him down. This strange rant would eventually become known as the "Son of Sam Letter".

Keep in mind that this bizarre missive was absolutely littered with misspellings and strange characterizations, and I am presenting it to you here just as Berkowitz wrote it. Without any correction or alteration, this is exactly how the letter read:

I am deeply hurt by your calling me a wemon hater. I am not. But I am not a monster. I am the 'Son of Sam.' I am a little brat. When Father Sam gets drunk he gets mean. He beats his family. Sometimes he ties me up to the back of the house. Other times he locks me in the garage. Sam loves to drink blood. 'Go out and kill' commands Father Sam. Behind our house some rest. Mostly young—raped and slaughtered—their blood drained—just bones now. Papa Sam keeps me locked in the attic, too. I can't get out but I look out the attic, too. I can't get out but I look out the attic window and watch the world go by. I feel like an outsider. I am on a different wave length then everybody else—programmed to kill. However, to stop me you must kill me. Attention all police: Shoot me first—shoot to kill or else. Keep out of my way or you will die! Papa Sam is old now. He needs some blood to preserve his youth. He has had too many heart attacks. Too many heart attacks. "Ugh, me hoot it urts sonny boy! I miss my pretty princess most of all. She's resting in our ladies house. But I'll she her soon. I am the 'monster'—Beelzebub. The Chubby Behemoth. I love to hunt. Prowling the streets looking for fair game—tasty meat. The wemon of Queens are z prettyist of all. I must be the water they drink. I live for the hunt—my life. Blood for Papa. Mr. Borelli, Sir, I don't want to kill anymore no sire, no more but I must, 'Honour thy Father'. I want to make love to the world. I love people. I don't belong on Earth. Return me to yahoos. To the people of Queens, I love you. And I want to wish all of you a happy Easter. May God bless you in this life and in the next. And for now I say goodbye and goodnight. POLICE: Let me haunt you with these words: I'll be back! I'll be back! To be interpreted as bang, bang, bang, bang, bang—ugh!! Yours in murder, Mr. Monster

At first, investigators didn't really know what to make of this odd letter. They simply wrote it off as the ramblings of a very deranged individual. But then different theories began to develop. Much attention was paid to the fact that the writer seemed to mimic a Scottish accent when saying that Papa Sam had "too many heart attacks". In this line of the letter, the writer seems to be speaking for Papa Sam by saying in his voice, "Ugh, me hoot it urts sonny boy". Taking this into consideration, some investigators wondered if the killer really was referencing his father, and whether he had a Scottish background. Some alternatively speculated that the killings were twisted acts of revenge because the killer's father had suffered from heart attacks and been mistreated by nurses at a local hospital. Those who took this line pointed out that one of the first victims was a medical technician and another was a nurse.

Such speculation is always something of a shot in the dark, and as it pertains to Berkowitz, it was decidedly off the mark. Sam was indeed a real person, but he was Berkowitz's neighbor Sam Carr, not his father. The description of the Son of Sam being tied up behind the house turned out to refer to Sam's black Labrador Retriever, which Berkowitz believed was speaking to him and telling him to kill.

But conspiracy theorists are, of course, perfectly content to continue speculating, and some of those who believe that Sam Carr's sons John and Michael were involved in the killings wonder whether Berkowitz even wrote the letter. Perhaps John or Michael Carr—a true blue "Son of Sam"—wrote it and told Berkowitz to drop it off at the scene of his next murder. The letter looks like it was created in a print shop, and coincidentally enough Sam Carr owned a print shop that he operated with his sons.

Whether it was manufactured in the Carr family print shop or not, this first strange letter was joined by a follow-up of sorts on May 30, 1977, when Jimmy Breslin, a *Daily News* columnist who had been following the case of the .44 Caliber Killer closely, received a letter from an individual claiming to be that very killer. The letter read:

Hello from the gutters of NYC which are filled with dog manure, vomit, stale wine, urine and blood. Hello from the sewers of NYC which swallow up these delicacies when they are washed away by the sweeper trucks. Hello from the cracks in the sidewalks of NYC and from the ants that dwell in these cracks and feed in the dried blood of the dead that has settled into the cracks. J.B., I'm just dropping you a line to let you know that I appreciate your interest in those recent and horrendous .44 killings. I also want to tell you that I read your column daily and I find it quite informative. Tell me Jim, what will you have for July twenty-ninth? You can forget about me if you like because I don't care for publicity. However you must not forget Donna Lauria and you cannot let the people forget her either. She was a very, very sweet girl but Sam's a thirsty lad and he won't let me stop killing until he gets his fill of blood. Mr. Breslin, sir, don't think that because you haven't heard from me for a while that I went to sleep. No, rather, I am still here. Like a spirit roaming the night. Thirsty, hungry, seldom stopping to rest; anxious to please Sam. I love my work. Now, the void has been filled. Perhaps we shall meet face to face someday or perhaps I will be blown away by cops with smoking .38's. Whatever, if I shall be fortunate enough to meet you I will tell you all about Sam if you like and I will introduce you to him. His name is 'Sam the terrible.' Not knowing what the future holds I shall say farewell and I will see you at the next job. Or should I say you will see my handiwork at the next job? Remember Ms. Lauria. Thank you. In their blood and from the gutter 'Sam's creation' .44. Here are some names to help you along. Forward them to the inspector for use by NCIC. 'The Duke of Death' 'The Wicked King Wicker' 'The Twenty Two Disciples of Hell' 'John Wheaties'—Rapist and Suffocator of Young Girls. PS: Please inform all the detectives working the slaying to remain. P.S.: J.B., Please inform all the detectives working the case that I wish them the best of luck. 'Keep 'em digging, drive on, think positive, get off your butts, knock on coffins, etc.' Upon my capture I promise to buy all the guys working the case a new pair of shoes if I can get up the money. Son of Sam.

Anyone who glances at these two letters can see some very obvious differences in style and penmanship. The first letter is riddled with simple punctuation and spelling errors, but the second seems to have a good grasp of grammar. This has led many to conclude that the two letters were written by two different people. Was this second letter actually written by the man nicknamed John Wheaties, Sam Carr's son John Carr? So far, no clear answers to this riddle are forthcoming.

Zeroing in on Berkowitz

After reviewing the taunting Breslin letter, the NYPD was desperate to find answers as to who the Son of Sam killer really was. That summer, they created a variety of elaborate ruses and traps to ensnare the killer, but none of them seemed to work. At one point they even sent out "decoy teams" of male and female officers and had them pretend to be making out in parked vehicles in order to attract the perpetrator. One can only imagine what a strange assignment this was for the officers involved, but in the end, it was all to no avail. The Son of Sam—whoever he might be—didn't rise to the bait.

And on June 25, 1977, the killing spree began anew. The victims this time around were 17-year-old Judy Placido and 20-year-old Salvatore Lupo. It was the weekend, and Judy had been hanging out with some of her friends at a disco in Queens. This was, of course, at the height of the disco era, and many a young person was getting their kicks under that shiny disco ball that night. Judy was having a good time, and just as her disco fever was beginning to break, she ran into Sal Lupo, a guy who really had a knack for busting a move on the dance floor. The two hit it off right away, and even when the clock struck two and her friends were ready to go home, Judy wanted to stay and hang out with Sal.

Like so many other young women hanging out in nightclubs, Judy had to make a decision: She could go home with her girlfriends or take a risk with an interesting guy. And although she had just met Sal, Judy trusted him and believed his promise that he would drive her home. Her friends were concerned about her, though, and the group broke into their own little huddle on the dance floor as Judy argued that she had nothing to fear from Sal. As it turned out, she was right: It would not be Sal, but an unknown figure from the shadows that would wreak terror on her that night.

After a lengthy discussion, Judy finally convinced her friends to let her stay with her new beau. After they left, she and Sal spent another good hour dancing under the disco ball before they decided to call it a night. Sal had to wait for his friend Saccate, who was a bouncer, to close up before he could leave, though, so he and Judy went out to his car to wait for him. *Honi soit qui mal y pense*; Sal behaved like a perfect gentleman, with his only move of physical affection being a casual arm placed over the back of Judy's seat as they discussed the current events of the day. The Son of Sam killings that were terrorizing the city were at the top of the list—and incredibly enough, the two were intently discussing just who this Son of Sam might be when the killer himself appeared before them and began shooting into their car!

The first bullet blasted through Sal's wrist, which had been resting around Judy's shoulder, before exiting and slicing through Judy's throat to finally lodge in the cushion of the car seat. Simultaneously, a piece of glass from the shattered window flew into Sal's thigh, creating a massive gash. Sal instinctively ducked down, but Judy was not so quick to react, and the next bullet struck her in the head. Fortunately, this one just grazed the skin of her brow. The mad gunman wasn't finished yet, though. He kept firing away, sending a third bullet through the girl's shoulder. By this point Sal had had enough. He popped open the driver's side door and fled for his life, leaving Judy to fend for herself.

Judy was pretty much out of it by this point. She wasn't sure what was happening, and it wasn't until she happened to see her refection in the rear-view mirror that she realized she was covered in blood. When she saw that grisly sight, the true horror of what was transpiring set in, and she quickly decided that Sal had had the right idea. She wrenched open the passenger side door and practically fell out of the car before beginning to make her way back to the glaring neon lights of the nightclub. She didn't have quite enough strength left, however, and she ended up passing out some distance away. This time, at least, there were some good Samaritans around: A group of passersby saw her distress and covered her with a blanket until paramedics arrived.

Sal, meanwhile, had run into the nightclub to enlist the brawn of his bouncer friend, but the killer was already long gone by the time they returned. Both Sal and Judy were taken to the hospital, Sal for injuries to his wrist and leg, and Judy for much more serious gunshot wounds to the head. Judy's prognosis was grim at first, but fortunately she pulled through and eventually made a full recovery.

Police quickly scrambled to the area in which the shooting had taken place. A few blocks away, they found a man who claimed to have seen a "stocky white male clad in dark clothing running along 211th Street," away from the location of the attack. Another witness, however, claimed to have seen a "well-dressed young man with sandy colored hair and a mustache jump into a yellow or gold Chevy Nova type of car" and drive around with the headlights off at the exact same time—and this description actually fits the profile of John Carr. Could this mustachioed man with sandy hair have been Berkowitz's accomplice that night? The mystery endures to this very day.

The Last Known Son of Sam Killings

The date of July 29, 1977, was a grim occasion for the citizens of New York City. This day marked the one-year anniversary of the first Son of Sam killing.

The night before this ominous anniversary, the woman who would be the final victim of the rampage, 21-year-old Stacy Moskowitz, was eating with her little sister Ricki at a diner called Beefsteak Charlie's. She had just returned from an excursion to Mexico and was full of fun and adventure. She was animatedly discussing her trip with her sister when she met Robert Violante. Robert was just 20 years old but brimming with confidence as he chatted up the girls in the restaurant, and he ended up sitting at their table to have dinner with them. He and Stacy hit it off, and the two exchanged phone numbers and agreed to go out together. They just had to pick a time, and perhaps they had the dreaded date of July 29th in mind when they picked the day after for their next liaison.

So it was just before 10 on the night of July 30th that the pair went to see *New York, New York* at the theater. After the show, they decided to go for a drive around the city. Feeling more and more comfortable with each other, they then made the fateful decision to make a pit stop at Shore Parkway, across from a baseball field and a city park, a place that was considered a sort of "lover's lane". Noting the late hour, they made sure to park under a streetlight, but its illumination would not help them when Berkowitz approached.

The couple were passionately making out in the car when he walked up to Stacy's side and began to fire his gun. In the ensuing barrage, both Stacy and Robert received bullets to the head. The gunman took off immediately after unleashing these missiles of death. Of the two victims, Robert was in better shape; he was actually cognizant enough to check on Stacy, who appeared to be much the worse for wear. He could hear her moaning in pain, but he couldn't see clearly, since the bullet that struck him had destroyed his left eye and significantly affected his right.

Not sure what else to do, Robert lay on his car horn to get the attention of anyone in the area. He knew that Stacy was fading fast and would bleed to death if she didn't get help soon. When no one responded to the horn, he stepped out of the vehicle and hung onto the nearby streetlight for support as he screamed for help at the top of his lungs. Hearing his cries, bystanders called an ambulance and the couple was taken to nearby Coney Island Hospital.

Stacy was conscious when admitted, but she was in rough shape, moaning pitifully in agony from her painful wounds. She had lost a lot of blood and needed immediate surgery to staunch this flow. Sadly, it was not enough; Stacy would ultimately pass away from her injuries. Although Robert survived, he would be blind in one eye for the rest of his life.

Berkowitz had gotten sloppy during this latest—and last—assault, however. Unlike the other attacks, this one produced plenty of eyewitnesses. And one of them, Tommy Zaino, had seen the entire thing play out. Tommy was parked three vehicles ahead of Robert and Stacy's car, and by sheer coincidence he was looking into his rearview mirror when the shooting started. Tommy saw the shooter as he fired his weapon, clearly illuminated under the "streetlight and full moon". The man was about 5'8" and around 28 years old, and he appeared to be wearing a wig.

If that's true, it could explain the discrepancies in Berkowitz's hair color in previous eyewitness testimony. And the notion that a wig was used was seconded by another witness to the latest attack who saw "a white male [who was wearing] a light-colored, cheap nylon wig" run from the scene, hop into a "small, light colored" vehicle and speed away. Remarking to her boyfriend that the man looked as if he had just "robbed a bank", she tried to write down his license plate number. However, she only managed to get the first four characters—either "4-GUR" or "4-GVR", she wasn't sure which.

Shortly after this, a motorist driving through the area almost collided with a yellow Volkswagen that ran a red light. In a report recorded under the pseudonym "Alan Masters", he told police how both cars hit the brakes before the other driver screamed a profanity and drove off. Masters, succumbing to a spate of full-on road rage, chased after the reckless driver. After several twists and turns, however, the other driver managed to shake him from his tail, and Masters gave up the pursuit. He described his antagonist as a white male in his late 20s with "high cheekbones, a narrow face, a cleft chin, very dark eyes, and messy, stringy" long hair.

Neither the description of the vehicle nor that of its driver matches with Berkowitz and his Ford Galaxie, and naturally this has only added more fuel to the conspiracy theories stating that there was more than one gunman at work in the Son of Sam slayings. This incident would be the last of those slayings, but the question still remains—which Son of Sam was it that pulled the trigger?

The Capture

David Berkowitz's reign of terror did not end with a dramatic standoff or a violent shootout. In effect, it ended with a parking ticket.

When he went out to shoot Stacy Moskowitz and Robert Violante, Berkowitz had parked too close to a fire hydrant. A woman named Cacilia Davis just happened to be taking her dog for a walk when she saw an officer placing a ticket on Berkowitz's windshield. Shortly thereafter, she saw the owner of the car—Berkowitz himself. She didn't like the looks of him, so she went back into her house. A few moments later, she heard the shots that slammed into Robert and Stacy's car.

A few days later, Cacilia reported the incident and Berkowitz became a person of interest—not so much as a suspect, but as a potential witness. The NYPD knew that Berkowitz was residing in Yonkers, so on August 9th, Detective James Justis called up the Yonkers Police Department to ask them to set up a meeting with Berkowitz. Coincidentally, his call was answered by none other than Sam Carr's daughter Wheat Carr, who happened to be working as a civilian police dispatcher!

The conversation went as follows:

WHEAT CARR: Police Headquarters.
JAMES JUSTIS: Yes, this is Detective Justis from the Brooklyn Robbery Squad. I'm trying to contact a party that lives up in Yonkers who is possibly a witness to the crime down here. That's a Mr. David Berkowitz.
WHEAT CARR: Oh no... Oh no...
JAMES JUSTIS: Do you know him?

WHEAT CARR: Could I... I was very involved. This is the guy that I think is responsible.
JAMES JUSTIS: Do you know David Berkowitz yourself?
WHEAT CARR: I don't know him. I really—because of a shooting incident at my home and a firebombing and threatening letters...
JAMES JUSTIS: At your home...
WHEAT CARR: ...and through investigation found out that this is probably the person.
JAMES JUSTIS: Did you notify the Police Department on it?
WHEAT CARR: Oh, yeah, there are numerous reports on it, and information regarding this guy was given to your department on Saturday.
JAMES JUSTIS: Yeah, well, I am doing it another way. He got a summons down here that night, right in the vicinity...
WHEAT CARR: Oh my God... he... he... you know, because we have seen him and he fits the description. This is why my father went down there with his whole file of copies of letters we have received from him. And I believe the Westchester County Sheriff's Department is now investigating him because he threatened a sheriff's investigator... My dog was shot with a .44 caliber bullet.
JAMES JUSTIS: Oh, really?
WHEAT CARR: At least that's what it was supposed to have been. The people who have seen it claim it was a .44.
JAMES JUSTIS: Ah.
WHEAT CARR: He... He just scared me to death... Now you are telling me he's a witness?
JAMES JUSTIS: Well, we don't know. A possible witness. And from what you're telling me, a possible perpetrator.

This strange phone conversation seems to indicate either a rather fortuitous moment for police—or the workings of a strange and elaborate plot. Detective Justis initially just wanted to question Berkowitz as a witness, but after a brief conversation with Wheat Carr, he saw him as the prime suspect. Furthermore, it is difficult to square what Wheat told Detective Justis with Berkowitz's later claims that he didn't act alone. In fact, it's impossible. Wheat's and Berkowitz's descriptions of his interactions with the Carr family tell two entirely different stories.

Wheat's testimony corroborates the theory that Berkowitz was simply a deranged psychopath who acted alone. She does not say that her family was friends with Berkowitz or had any other association with him. According to her, he was just some weird guy who lived nearby, became obsessed with her dad and his dog, and began to harass them by leaving bizarre letters and trying to kill the dog on one occasion.

Berkowitz, on the other hand, told an elaborate tale in which he and John and Michael Carr were not only friends but active coreligionists in a satanic cult that practiced animal sacrifices and other dark rituals. Unless Wheat's brothers successfully managed to keep their dark dealings with Berkowitz secret from her, there are only two possibilities—either Wheat is lying, or Berkowitz is.

If Berkowitz really was the fall guy for the Carrs' satanic cult, Wheat certainly crafted an excellent narrative to put the blame all on Berkowitz's shoulders. But whatever the truth of the matter, it was her conversation with Detective Justis that led to Berkowitz's capture. Because as soon as he put down the phone, the detective changed his mind about interviewing Berkowitz and instead ordered a stakeout of his apartment.

On the following evening, August 10th, a group of detectives showed up outside Berkowitz's residence in Yonkers. Finding his Ford Galaxie outside the apartment complex, they searched the vehicle and discovered a rifle in the back, along with a duffel bag of ammunition. Even more incriminating were maps of several crime scenes and a threatening letter addressed to Inspector

Timothy Dowd, who headed the special task force assigned to the Son of Sam case.

Although the police didn't yet have a search warrant for Berkowitz's apartment, they knew they could let him get away. They decided to set up shop outside and confront him when he came out, but these plans hit a small snag when a volunteer deputy name Craig Glassman, who lived in the same apartment building, decided to snoop around his suspicious neighbor's car. Not realizing that the vehicle was under police surveillance, he walked right up to it and began looking inside. The watching detectives, assuming that he was Berkowitz, left their positions further down the street and quickly approached him with guns drawn. But before they reached him, Deputy Glassman had already satisfied his curiosity and turned to walk back up to his apartment.

Still thinking that they had their man, one of the detectives shouted, "Hey, Dave! Dave! Hold on a minute!" When Deputy Glassman turned around to see what all the fuss was about, he was confronted by a host of policemen pointing guns in his direction. Fortunately, he was a quick thinker. He put two and two together and realized that they were after his strange neighbor David Berkowitz, then raised his hands and yelled, "I'm not David! I'm not David!" After he showed them his driver's license, they grudgingly agreed and let him go.

With all the commotion it was a wonder that Berkowitz, still holed up in his high-rise apartment, wasn't alerted to the drama. Nevertheless, he apparently didn't suspect anything when he finally came out of the apartment at around 10 o'clock and headed for his car. The police were still waiting for him, and before he could even start the engine of the Ford Galaxie, detectives John Falotico and William Gardella got the drop on him. With one of them on each side of the car, they aimed their weapons squarely at Berkowitz's head and let him know that he was under arrest.

Berkowitz didn't seem fazed by this at all. In fact, he seemed as if he had been expecting it. This has led some to theorize that he had been tipped off ahead of time—but of course it's equally possible that he was simply suffering from a guilty conscience. In any event, he wasn't alarmed at his arrest in the slightest. If anything, he seemed relieved that the police had finally moved in. His words to the arresting officers were shockingly mild. Staring down the barrels of their guns, he gently stated, "Well, you got me. How come it took such a long time?"

Sam on Trial

Police conducted a preliminary interview of David Berkowitz almost as soon as they got their hands on him. It began just after three in the morning of August 11th and lasted about half an hour. The interrogation was "off the record", but Berkowitz allegedly held fast to the narrative that he was told to commit his crimes by a demonic entity that inhabited his neighbor Sam Carr's dog. He also intimated that he believed that Sam himself was a "six-thousand-year-old man" immersed in the dark arts of necromancy. However, he maintained that his primary motivation for the murders was to satiate Sam's demon dog, which continually "demanded the blood of pretty young girls".

Some who subscribe to the theory that Berkowitz was chosen as the fall guy by other members of his satanic cult have postulated that he was carefully laying the foundation for an insanity plea with these bizarre assertions. Investigative journalist Terry Maury literally wrote the book on such conspiratorial musings, and in his epic piece entitled *The Ultimate Evil*, he asserts that Berkowitz was told by other cult members to come up with such crazy stories so that he could be found "not guilty by reason of insanity". Maury theorizes that the cultists persuaded Berkowitz to take the rap by convincing him that he would probably just be placed in a mental institution for a few years and then released. (Or maybe they promised to break him out.) Maury believes that Berkowitz was simply following this prearranged game plan.

Of course, the simpler and more widely accepted explanation is that Berkowitz really was out of his mind and actually believed all the strange things he was saying. If he was indeed hearing voices in his head—whether from demons or his own shattered subconscious mind—who knows what insanities they were speaking.

At any rate, the police were satisfied that they had their man, and Mayor Beame quickly announced that the Son of Sam had been caught. Shortly afterward, Berkowitz was thoroughly evaluated by a panel of psychologists to make sure that he was fit to stand trial. And if Berkowitz was looking for a way out of court by feigning insanity, he failed; he would indeed stand trial for the crimes that he was accused of. Even so, his attorneys advised him to enter a plea of "not guilty by reason of insanity".

Interestingly enough, Berkowitz demurred and insisted on pleading guilty as charged, which he did in a court appearance on May 8, 1978. The court promptly accepted the plea, but the sentencing hearing proved to be a little more dramatic. First, Berkowitz got free from his handlers and attempted to leap out of a window on the 7th floor of the courthouse. He was caught before he could, but no sooner had order been restored than he began to mock his final victim, Stacy Moskowitz, by chanting over and over in a low but audible voice, "Stacy was a whore." Stacy's relatives were understandably enraged and began screaming at Berkowitz. At this point the judge gave up and decided to postpone the hearing to a later date.

So it wasn't until June 12th that Berkowitz received his sentence—25 to life, for every life he had admitted to snuffing out. Incredibly enough, this left the door open for the possibility of parole after his first 25 years—but everyone knew that the odds of Berkowitz ever receiving it were well-nigh insurmountable.

Berkowitz was shipped off to New York's notorious Attica maximum security prison. It was notorious for its violence, and just one year into his sentence, Berkowitz was nearly killed by one of his fellow inmates. The attacker, whose identity has just recently been revealed as William E. Hauser, apparently got hold of a razor, sneaked up behind Berkowitz, and expertly slit his throat. The wound was as severe as it sounds, and if Berkowitz had not been attended to immediately, he would surely have perished—but amazingly, he was able to walk himself to the nearby prison infirmary. Several stitches later, the bleeding had stopped and his life had been saved.

Hauser was never charged with the assault; Berkowitz refused to press charges and the matter was dropped. Adherents to the satanic cult theory speculate that the cult had ordered Hauser to assassinate their fall guy Berkowitz after he failed to go along with the planned insanity defense. But Berkowitz himself believed that the man was simply trying to "make a name for himself" by taking out the Son of Sam killer. Berkowitz didn't hold the attack against Hauser; in fact, he even claimed to feel grateful for it, saying that it was "the punishment I deserve".

Even without someone else trying to kill him, Berkowitz was quite suicidal at the time, and on at least one occasion he did attempt to take his own life. As nebulous as his time before prison was, his first few years of incarceration would prove to be the darkest of his life. The days were long, and the nights even longer, and with about 300 years' worth of prison time to serve, Berkowitz began to feel that he could not go on. Even so, he still tried to find some light at the end of the tunnel, some small vestige of hope despite all of his misery and pain.

The Son of Sam Becomes the Son of Hope

David Berkowitz, as he tells it, was a man of complete despair and hopelessness. But all that changed one cold winter night out in the prison yard in the late 1980s when a fellow inmate began to reach out and minister to him about the redemptive faith of Christianity. Of course, Berkowitz had already dabbled in Christianity as a young man in the Army, but he had quickly discounted this period as a mere passing phase in his life. He figured that he had tried it—and it had failed him just like everything else.

But his fellow inmate was persistent, and he preached in a way that Berkowitz wasn't familiar with. In the past, he had known preachers to spew fiery sermons from the pulpit about God's wrath and judgment. He had learned quite a bit about that, and he figured that by now—several murders later—he was most definitely on God's bad side. But this man explained the nature of God's forgiveness in a way that no one had before. He told Berkowitz that Jesus was willing to forgive man of all sins, big and small, if he would just believe in him.

At first, Berkowitz openly mocked and ridiculed this incarcerated zealot. But the man—whom Berkowitz has identified only as "Rick"—refused to give up, sticking to him like a piece of proselytizing glue. Every time Berkowitz went out to the prison yard, there was Rick, preaching away. He was serious about his beliefs and never tired of telling Berkowitz that God would be willing to erase the past and let him start anew, with a clean slate, if he would just accept Christ's forgiveness and turn from his wicked ways. The more Berkowitz heard this message being preached, the less ridiculous and the more appealing it sounded.

Soon he was debating with Rick about religion and what it meant to be a Christian. His conversion finally came in late 1987, when he was alone in his cell reading from the Book of Psalms. It was when he came across Psalm 34 and read the words "this poor man cried, and the Lord heard him, and saved him from all his troubles" that he felt that God was really speaking to him. Yet again, Berkowitz was having a supernatural experience—but of the God kind, not the satanic kind. He felt that the weight and burden of all of his pain, guilt, and sorrow had been miraculously lifted off of him by God.

On that cold winter night of 1987, Berkowitz spent several hours on his knees crying and praying to God. And when he finally got up, he says he felt like a different man: "When I got up it felt as if a very heavy but invisible chain that had been around me for so many years was broken. A Peace flooded over me. I did not understand what was happening. But in my heart, I just knew that my life, somehow, was going to be different."

Even so, Berkowitz admits that he was initially hesitant to acknowledge his newfound faith out in the prison yard. The next time he met Rick, he actually tried to conceal his conversion. But sometime later, he casually asked the prison preacher, "Hey, Rick, guess what I did the other night?"

Rick responded, "What did you do?"

Berkowitz then informed him, "I asked Jesus to come into my life."

Right there in the middle of the prison yard, Rick started to jump up and down and shout, "Praise the Lord!"

Berkowitz, eyeing some rather intimidating looking inmates strolling around the yard nearby, was afraid of bringing unwanted attention to themselves. He quickly tried to stifle Rick's praise, telling him, "Stop! Stop! Don't embarrass us!" Berkowitz already stood out among his peers, and he didn't want the target on his back to become any larger.

But Rick saw things differently. He saw that Berkowitz was in the middle of a kind of metamorphosis in which he was changing for the better. Through the previous darkness in Berkowitz's eyes, the prison preacher could see a faint glimmer of light beginning to shine. And regardless of who else was around at the time, Rick was ecstatic at the change that he perceived. He informed Berkowitz, "You don't understand. That means you have been born again. You're saved now! You're a new person!"

For Berkowitz, this confirmation confirmed his experience. Instead of casting it aside as a mere aberration, Berkowitz fully embraced the feeling of grace that seemed to well up from within. For the first time in his life, he felt that he had a future. Despite the horrendous crimes of the past, he had a path from which he could go forward. According to David Berkowitz, it was at this moment that he left the demonic Son of Sam behind and became the Son of Hope.

What Really Happened?

Many who have followed the Son of Sam killings find it very hard to accept that David Berkowitz actually acted alone. Yet at the same time, it's something of a stretch to believe that the wall of silence around the purported satanic conspiracy could really have held firm for all these years.

Whatever the truth may be, the surviving victims, the victims' families, and Berkowitz himself all contend that it doesn't really matter anyway. Berkowitz still admits to committing some of the murders and to being involved in the others. He regularly expresses remorse for all of his crimes and believes that—whether he killed all victims of the Son of Sam slayings or just three of them—life in prison is a just punishment for him.

Survivors and family members also realize that whether others were involved or not, it makes no difference when it comes to the tragic results. The damage has been done, long ago now. Berkowitz has said repeatedly that if he could go back in time and change what happened, he would. All we can do is take him at his word.

Further Readings

As I bring this book to a close, I would like to make mention of the reading and reference materials that helped me write it. In this appendix, you will find books, websites, and other resources related to various aspects of the Son of Sam case. If you would like to know a little more about any aspect of the story, please feel free to check them out for yourself.

Son of Sam. Lawrence D. Klauser
Coming out in the early 1980s, this was one of the first books about David Berkowitz. It was written before Berkowitz's claims of involvement with a satanic cult, so it doesn't address that aspect of the story. For the most part, Klauser's book paints a picture of Berkowitz as a lone, tormented individual who slipped into a dark fantasy world of madness. Much is made of Berkowitz's early statements to the press about his neighbor's dog communicating with him. Aside from its limited scope as to what may have driven Berkowitz, this book does an excellent job of chronicling all of Berkowitz's alleged assaults from the Christmas Eve stabbings of 1975 to his final murders in 1977.

The Ultimate Evil: An Investigation into a Dangerous Satanic Cult. Maury Terry
This book by investigative journalist Maury Terry was written in 1987, ten years after Berkowitz's arrest. Here you will find a good play-by-play of the Son of Sam killings as well as an excellent background on Berkowitz himself. But beyond all of this, Terry's book—more than any other—lays out the groundwork for a possible satanic conspiracy. Terry connects the dots between the Carr family and Berkowitz better than anyone else before or since. If you would like to learn more about the conspiracy angle, this book is the one that you should have on your shelf.

www.cnn.com
The archives over at CNN are a great source of all kinds of information, and David Berkowitz is no exception. Of particular interest was an interview Berkowitz did with Larry King from prison. This interview provides some great insights on what motivated Berkowitz during his dark days of killing, and it also touches on his life in prison and his alleged conversion. You can find the transcript of this interview here on CNN's website.

www.cbn.com
Another noteworthy Berkowitz interview was done by CBN—the Christian Broadcasting Network. In the transcript, Berkowitz speaks at length about his prison conversion to Christianity.

www.youtube.com
YouTube, of course, has just about everything known to man, including some of the harder to find information on Berkowitz, from documentaries to the notorious 1993 *Inside Edition* interview.

www.ariseandshine.org
David Berkowitz's personal website presents his life story, his journal, an apology for his crimes, and a lot more. It's worth taking the time to read some of the articles Berkowitz wrote, as they show another side of this sordid story.

Image credits
Cover image
By M62 - Own work, CC BY-SA 3.0,
https://commons.wikimedia.org/w/index.php?curid=2518007

The Last Month of Mayhem
By Son of Sam - http://en.wikipedia.org/wiki/Image:1stsosletter.jpg, Public Domain,
https://commons.wikimedia.org/w/index.php?curid=1689116

Also by Jack Smith

Printed in Great Britain
by Amazon